Fact Finders®

See It,
Write It

# Picture Yourself
# *writing*
# NONFICTION

## Using **Photos** to **Inspire** Writing

by Jennifer Fandel

CAPSTONE PRESS
a capstone imprint

Fact Finders are published by Capstone Press,
151 Good Counsel Drive, P.O. Box 669, Mankato, Minnesota 56002.
www.capstonepub.com

Books published by Capstone Press are manufactured with paper
containing at least 10 percent post-consumer waste.

Library of Congress Cataloging-in-Publication Data
Fandel, Jennifer.
 Picture yourself writing nonfiction : using photos to inspire writing / by Jennifer Fandel.
 p. cm.—(Fact finders. see it, write it)
 Summary: "Useful tips and writing prompts show young writers how to use images to inspire
nonfiction writing"—Provided by publisher.
 Includes bibliographical references and index.
 ISBN 978-1-4296-6125-6 (library binding)
 ISBN 978-1-4296-7207-8 (paperback)
 1. Journalism—Authorship—Juvenile literature. 2. Report writing—Juvenile literature. 3. Photography—
Juvenile literature. I. Title.
 PN4776.F36 2012
 808'.042—dc22
                                                                    2011002116

**Editorial Credits**
Jennifer Besel, editor; Veronica Correia, designer; Eric Manske, production specialist

**Photo Credits**
Alamy: Asianet-Pakistan/Owais Aslam Ali, 20; AP Images: Phil Coale, cover, 1; Corbis: Bettmann, 17
(bottom right); Dreamstime: Erwinova, 13; Getty Images Inc.: AFP/Alexander Joe, 14, Joe Raedle, 27,
Keystone, 17 (top); iStockphoto: clu, 22, Jasna Hrovatin, 9, Jodi Jacobson, 5, Leif Norman, 26, Liz
Leyden, 24, Sharon Dominick, 10; Library of Congress, Prints & Photographs Division, 19, FSA/OWI
Collection, 6; NARA, 3, 17 (bottom left); Photo courtesy of Jennifer Fandel, 32; PhotoEdit Inc.: Paul
Conklin, 7; Shutterstock: beltsazar, 8, Dariusz Kantorski, 12, David W. Leindecker, 23, Juriah Mosin,
18, Maria Gioberti, 25, NicolasMcComber, 15, ollirg, 28-29, Richard Seeley, 16, Rui Alexandre
Araujo, 21, Seleznev Oleg, 11

Printed in the United States of America in Stevens Point, Wisconsin.
032011      006111WZF11

# TABLE OF CONTENTS

# Nothing but the Truth

Have you ever heard the phrase "truth is stranger than fiction?"

Strange and exciting things happen every day. With such good stuff to write about, there's no need to make things up!

Nonfiction writing focuses on facts. It has characters, setting, **plot**, and many other fiction qualities. But nonfiction authors use real people, real places, and real events as their subjects.

Nonfiction can take many forms. News stories provide factual reports. **Narratives** show readers new places and dangerous situations. Diaries and memoirs give readers a glimpse into people's lives.

Photos are nonfiction events frozen in time. They can show you what happened in a specific place. Or they could remind you of personal experiences. With a photo, you're never far from a great nonfiction idea. Let the world of nonfiction take flight.

**plot**—the main story of a piece of writing

**narrative**—an account of something that has happened

## The Writing Process

### Step 1 Prewrite

Plan what you're going to write. Are you going to write a nonfiction story, a poem, or some other form of writing? Choose a topic, and start brainstorming details. Also identify your audience and the purpose of your piece.

### Step 2 Draft

Put your ideas on paper. Start crafting your composition. Don't worry about getting the punctuation and grammar perfect. Just start writing.

## Step 4 Edit

Now look for those pesky punctuation errors. Also check your spelling, grammar, and capitalization.

## Step 3 Revise

Check your work for ways to improve your writing. Fix areas that are confusing. Look for spots that need reorganizing. Are there places where you could make the words more clear or exciting? Having other people look at your work might be helpful too.

## Step 5 Publish

When you're done, share your work! You can present it to a class or post it online. Maybe you could have it printed in your school newspaper. The possibilities for sharing your work are endless.

# Chapter 1

# DETAILING THE FACTS

## Gathering Facts

Nonfiction writing is all about presenting facts. That means you'll need to research. A photo is a good place to start. Photos show a moment in time. The photo **caption** provides some key information about that moment. Then dig into reliable **sources** to learn as much about your topic as you can.

### As you research, try to answer these six key questions:

**WHO:** Florence Owens Thompson and her children

**WHAT:** migrant farm laborer and mother

**WHEN:** 1936

**WHERE:** California

**WHY DID SHE LIVE THIS WAY:** During the Dust Bowl, many farmers lost their farms and moved to California to find work.

**HOW DID THIS WOMAN LIVE:** She and her family survived on killed birds and vegetables frozen in fields.

**Finally, weave together the facts to create a powerful nonfiction piece.**

*It was 1936, and the hardships of the Dust Bowl hit Florence Owens Thompson's family hard. She was a migrant farm laborer in California. She and her children survived on birds they killed for food and vegetables they found frozen in fields.*

Florence Thompson with three of her children in a photograph known as "Migrant Mother"

**caption**—a description printed below a photograph

**source**—something that provides information, such as books or Web sites

# Write about It!

Let this photo inspire a story about the memorial. Do some research about the Vietnam War and the people who fought in it. Make sure to find the answers to the six key questions. Then use those facts in a paragraph about the memorial.

A veteran visits the Vietnam Veterans Memorial in Washington, D.C. The war lasted from 1959–1975.

# Sensory Details

## We experience the world through our five senses.

The best writing uses those **sensory** experiences to make nonfiction facts come to life. Try to use details for at least three senses in every paragraph.

Details in photos can trigger ideas for sensory details. Make a chart of sensory details to start re-creating the moment. Put five columns on a piece of paper, labeled with the five senses. Then fill it in!

| Sight | arms everywhere; puffy sleeves on the costumes; they look steady on the bike |
| Sound | "ta-da" music of the horns; quiet gasp of disbelief |
| Touch | the warmth of the spotlight |
| Smell | popcorn; sawdust |
| Taste | sweet drinks; roasted peanuts |

### ONCE YOU HAVE YOUR SENSORY DETAILS, WEAVE THEM INTO YOUR WRITING.

The smell of popcorn hung in the air. One by one, the performers piled onto the bike. It seemed impossible. When finally the bike was a blur of puffy sleeves, the horns sounded a final "ta-da!" There was a quiet gasp of disbelief as the acrobats circled the circus ring.

sensory—having to do with the five senses

# Write about It!

Let this photo help you remember an experience you've had with birds or any other animal. What sound did the animals make? How did they smell? Make a chart of sensory details. Then write a paragraph using your details. Dare yourself to use all of the senses. Make your experience come alive for readers.

9

# Unique Comparisons

Presenting information in a surprising way will also engage readers. **Similes** and **metaphors** are unique tools that show readers new ways of seeing and experiencing the world.

Photos can inspire **SIMILES** in your writing. Look at this ear of corn. Can you think of fresh, exciting ways to describe this everyday item?

> corn silk like soft hair

> kernels like teeth

Similes are interesting. But **METAPHORS** will surprise readers even more. Metaphors don't just compare the items, they call items something else.

> the corn silk is soft hair

> the kernels are teeth

**NOW THAT'S A METAPHOR WITH BITE!**

**simile**—a way of describing something by comparing it with something else; similes use the words "like" or "as"

**metaphor**—a way of describing something by calling it something else

10

# write about It!

Make a list of sensory details about this lizard. Then use the list to create surprising similes. What are its eyes like? What does its skin remind you of? How about the way he's stretching? Once you have a list of 10 similes, turn five of the similes into metaphors. Pick your best similes and metaphors, and use them in a paragraph about the lizard.

11

# Chapter 2

# THE PEOPLE

## characters

Nonfiction characters are real people with real thoughts, feelings, and problems.

Interviews are the best way to research characters. In an interview, start with the six key questions.

| | |
|---|---|
| Who are you? | Toby Smith |
| What do you do? | build pipelines for the oil industry |
| When did you start? | 10 years ago |
| Where do you work? | all over the state of Louisiana |
| Why do you do this work? | "I like the challenge and danger." |
| How? | Safety equipment lowers him deep into the pipes. |

Take notes on what you observe during an interview. How does the person move, sound, talk, and look?

- **His voice is rough, but quiet.**
- **His hands have cuts from holding the safety rope.**
- **Question: "Are you worried about the danger of your job?" He looks down. He says his family worries.**

To make real people come alive on the page, you need a mixture of facts and details.

Toby Smith's hands are covered with cuts. The cuts are from holding the safety rope as he is lowered deep into pipes. He's built pipelines for Louisiana's oil industry for 10 years. "I like the challenge and danger," he says in his rough, quiet voice. But he looks down when he says how much his family worries.

# write about It!

Use this photo as inspiration for an interview with someone who works with food. Prepare questions using the six key question words. What do you want to know about this person and his or her job? During the interview, be sure to write down sensory details about the person.

After the interview write a paragraph describing the character you interviewed. Make this person come alive right before your readers' eyes.

13

# Dialogue

Dialogue in nonfiction allows readers to hear characters speak. Dialogue can come from your interviews.

Interviewing, like writing, is a skill that takes time to master. The more interviews you do, the better you'll get. Here are a few tips to help you get started.

· Always be prepared. Bring a list of questions that you want answered.
· Ask follow up questions. If the person says something you want to know more about, ask.

· Do an audio recording. With a recording you can go back later and check the **quotations** you use.

If you can't get an interview, dialogue can come from speeches or videos. No matter where they come from, present quotations carefully in your writing. Include answers to the six key questions. The facts will help keep the quotation **in context**.

| | | |
|---|---|---|
| · **Who** said it? | · **When** was it said? | · **Why** was it said? |
| · **What** was said? | · **Where** was it said? | · **How** was it said? |

South African leader Nelson Mandela giving a speech on September 20, 1990.

The crowd was excited to witness this moment. Many of these South Africans had just voted for the first time. They had elected Nelson Mandela as their president.

In his inauguration address, Mandela said, "We understand it still that there is no easy road to freedom."

His voice was firm but gentle. He did not smile. He wanted the people to know there was still much work to be done.

**quotation**—a part of an interview that is repeated as it was originally said
**in context**—taking into account the events and actions surrounding a statement

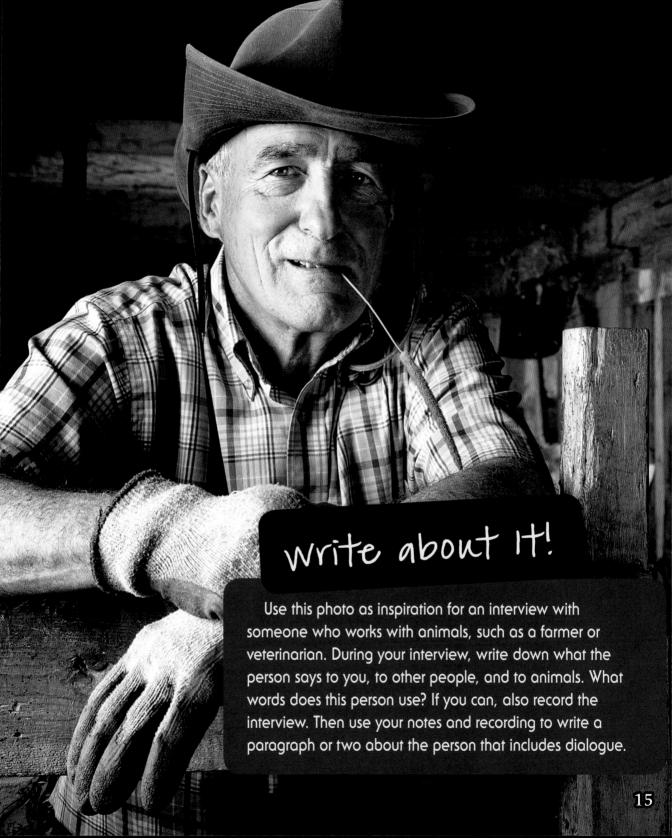

# write about It!

Use this photo as inspiration for an interview with someone who works with animals, such as a farmer or veterinarian. During your interview, write down what the person says to you, to other people, and to animals. What words does this person use? If you can, also record the interview. Then use your notes and recording to write a paragraph or two about the person that includes dialogue.

# Chapter 3

# PLACING THE ACTION

## Plot

A photo shows one moment of action—one piece of a story's plot. You'll have to research to find out what happened before and after that moment.

Look at this photo of a bear fishing. Use your research skills to outline the events that came before and after this event.

Outlining is a great prewriting tool. It helps make sure you have events in the right order.

1. In October, the weather turns cold. The bear eats as much as it can. One of its key foods is salmon.

2. In November the bear finds a den and begins hibernating.

3. In February increased sunlight warms the earth, waking the bear.

4. The bear leaves its den and wanders through the snow to look for food.

The next step is to turn your plot outline into paragraphs. Instead of numbering the steps in the plot, use transition words. Transition words alert readers to changes. They also keep the order of your story clear. Here are just a few transition words:

- then
- next
- finally
- after
- before
- later

The cool October weather has salmon on the move. Finally, the giant bear has eaten his fill. It lumbers to its den to sleep.

pilot Paul Tibbets Jr. before takeoff in the bomber that would drop the atomic bomb on Hiroshima

# Write about It!

These three photos show events related to World War II (1939–1945). First use your observation and research skills to learn the stories behind the pictures. Then make an outline of the events that connect these photos. Finally, write a story based on these events. Use transition words to move from event to event.

the atomic bomb explosion in Nagasaki, Japan

A Japanese child is left in the rubble after the atomic bomb explosion in Hiroshima on August 6, 1945.

# Setting

## All **stories** take **place** in a **setting.**

Unlike fiction, nonfiction is set in a real place and in a real time—just like a photo.

This photo provides plenty of details about the setting. But to get the whole story, you have to research. Where is this woman? What is she doing?

Readers won't always see the pictures that inspire you. You need to describe a setting so readers see the picture in their minds. Use sensory details, active verbs, **concrete nouns**, and sharp adjectives to describe the setting.

Choosing just the right words is important. You could say this woman is in a boat. But the description is more active if you say her boat drifts on the water. Concrete nouns help readers get the specifics. The woman is selling fruit, but describing the star fruit would be more engaging.

A local woman sells fresh produce at Damnoen Saduak floating market in Bangkok, Thailand.

The old woman lives in Bangkok, Thailand. She makes her living in this busy tourist town by selling fresh star fruit and melons. The plump, juicy fruits fill her long, narrow boat as she drifts on the still water.

**concrete noun**—a specific person, place, or thing that vividly points to a particular item

# write about It!

Make a list of everything you notice in this photo. Are there any clues about the location? Do you notice anything that would hint at the time period? Using your list of details and research skills, figure out where this photo was taken. Then write a paragraph that puts readers in this setting. Use active verbs, concrete nouns, and sharp adjectives to describe what you see in the photo.

# Scene

## A **scene** shows what **happens** in a single **setting.**

To create a scene, describe a moment with facts and sensory details. Let's create a scene from this photo. We'll start with details from the photo.

*Water is everywhere. People stand on a rooftop, waiting to be rescued. A rescuer holds on to the man's head, protecting him, as they are pulled up by a helicopter.*

Army officials rescue people stranded by the flood in Sukkur, Pakistan.

Then do research to gather facts about this scene.

**WHO** is affected? 20,000 people in Pakistan

**WHAT** is happening? People are being rescued by Pakistan's army.

**WHEN:** summer 2010

**WHERE:** throughout much of Pakistan

**WHY:** Monsoon rains caused flooding on the rivers.

**HOW** did the rescues work: Rescuers from the army airlifted people out by helicopter.

Now weave details and facts together as if you're a tour guide showing people around the scene.

*During the summer of 2010, water was everywhere in Pakistan. In the city of Sukkur, people had waited for help on rooftops for days. Finally, the wind whipped overhead as rescuers from the Pakistani Army arrived in a helicopter.*

# write about It!

Use this photo to inspire a scene. You could research this exact match or one that's closer to home. Make a list of sensory details that describe the scene. Then research to find out some background information. Finally, write a paragraph using the details and facts to create the scene. Remember to describe everything carefully to make your readers feel like they are in the middle of the action.

soccer match between Portugal and Ukraine on September 28, 2010

21

# Chapter 4

# PRESENTING THE TRUTH

## Purpose and Audience

When you begin a writing project, you'll need to decide on a purpose and audience.

Purpose is the reason you are writing. Do you want to inform readers? Make them laugh? Change their minds? A clear purpose makes it easier to pick the facts and details to include. For example, emotional details about losing a pet would work well in a personal narrative but not in a news report.

You write for an audience. Are your readers young or old? What kinds of activities do they like? What is their background? Imagine speaking to your audience when choosing details and facts. Pick information your readers will understand. In a story meant for senior citizens, would you choose skateboarding as an example of exercise?

Check out this example. What's the purpose? Who would be interested in this nonfiction piece?

*I could hardly see. I had stacked so many books in my arms. I walked carefully and slowly—right into a glass wall! My books flew everywhere, and I landed on top of them. The librarian looked up from her glasses. "Shush," she said.*

# write about It!

Use this photo to jump-start ideas for a news article. Once you have your idea, choose the audience you want to write for and your purpose. Then use details from the photo and research to write a short article.

When you're done, switch up your purpose. If you wrote an informational article, change it to a persuasive one. Use different facts and details to support this new purpose in another short article.

**persuasive**—having the ability to make someone do or believe something

23

# Point of View

In your **nonfiction**, you'll have to choose **who** will tell the **story**.

The way you present information is the story's **point of view** (POV). But remember that no matter who it is, the storyteller has to stick to the facts.

**1** A common POV in nonfiction is first person. When you write in first person, you tell *your* story. This POV is best for writing about your own experiences.

*I hung the bird feeder on a pole to keep the squirrels away. I was amazed to see the squirrel hang from his toes to eat.*

**2** You can also step into someone else's shoes—or paws! Some authors write first-person stories as if they were someone else. To do this, make sure the details you use show the other person's or animal's true thoughts—not your own.

*I saw the birdseed hanging from the pole. If you give me the choice of acorns or birdseed, I'll pick birdseed every time!*

**3** Third person is another common nonfiction POV. Third person presents a story as someone would see it from the outside. This POV is used most often in media reports.

*Squirrels are intelligent animals. The new poles to keep squirrels away don't work. Squirrels will risk falling headfirst if it means getting food.*

**point of view**—the way someone or something looks at or thinks about something

# write about It!

Write a paragraph about this musician's story. Before you begin, make a list of all of the details you notice in this photo. Then use these details to create a list of questions to research. Remember to use your six key question words: who, what, where, when, why, and how. Finally, combine your details and facts to write a third-person story. To make your writing stand out, think about what the musician might want readers to know.

musicians in Cape Town, South Africa

# Bias

## People have all kinds of differing opinions.

Good nonfiction reporting explores all sides of a topic. If only one opinion is told, the story is biased. In a biased report, readers only get one side of the story.

A picture of a protest could inspire you to write about an issue people are arguing about. In your writing, present all sides of the topic. Presenting all sides shows you've done your research and creates trust between you and your audience.

**BiASED REPORTiNG:** People are right to protest cuts in school budgets. The government needs to find money for schools. Every person I talked with agreed with me.

**UNBiASED REPORTiNG:** Cuts in school budgets are a big problem for communities. Without funding, many programs will be cut. But the government doesn't have enough money to fund everything.

Fair reporting starts with fair interviewing. Ask people questions that don't take sides. You wouldn't want to ask, "Why are you against a law that's good for schools?" Instead, ask neutral questions, such as

"How do you feel about this issue?"
"Why do you feel this way?"

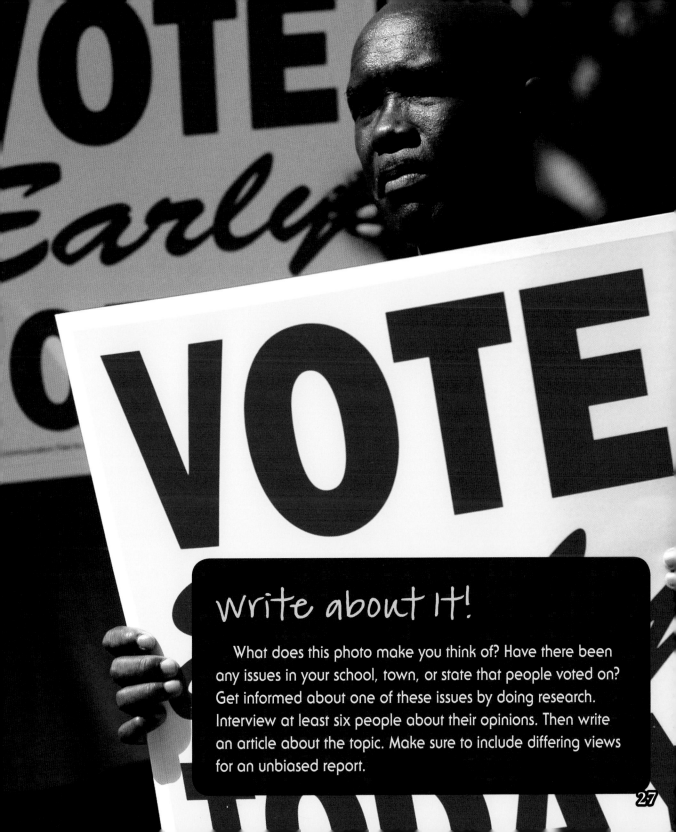

## Write about It!

What does this photo make you think of? Have there been any issues in your school, town, or state that people voted on? Get informed about one of these issues by doing research. Interview at least six people about their opinions. Then write an article about the topic. Make sure to include differing views for an unbiased report.

# Your Writing Journey

**Writing** nonfiction is like a **journey** to **new** worlds.

Photos are a great way to start your journey. They place you in the middle of a scene.

Suddenly there are tons of questions to ask. There are people to interview and characters to get to know. There are purposes and points of view to consider. There are reliable sources to find and places and times to research.

You can re-create a nonfiction world that is as real as the photo in your hand. Where will your nonfiction journey take you?

# write about It!

Using this picture as inspiration, list 10 journeys you've taken. Besides taking trips, think about going to a new school, moving to a new place, or gaining or losing a family member. Just about anything that teaches you about yourself or others can be a journey. Then pick one of these journeys to write about. Use all of the tools in your nonfiction toolbox to put readers right in the middle of your experience.

# GLOSSARY

**caption** (KAP-shuhn)—a description printed below a photograph

**concrete noun** (KON-kreet NOUN)—a specific person, place, or thing that vividly points to a particular item; the word dog is a general noun, while poodle is a concrete noun

**in context** (IN KON-tekst)—taking into account the events and actions surrounding a statement

**metaphor** (MET-uh-for)—a way of describing something by calling it something else

**narrative** (NA-ruh-tiv)—an account of something that has happened

**persuasive** (per-SWAY-siv)—having the ability to make someone do or believe something by giving good reasons

**plot** (PLOT)—the main story of a piece of writing

**point of view** (POINT UV VYOO)—the way someone or something looks at or thinks about something

**quotation** (kwoh-TAY-shuhn)—a part of an interview or speech that is repeated exactly as it was originally said

**sensory** (SEN-suh-ree)—having to do with the five senses

**simile** (SIM-uh-lee)—a way of describing something by comparing it with something else; similes use the words "like" or "as"

**source** (SORSS)—someone or something that provides information

# READ MORE

**Beutel, Roger and Lauren Spencer.** *Writing about Issues.* Write Like a Pro. New York: Rosen Pub., 2012.

**Gaines, Ann.** *Master the Library and Media Center.* Ace It! Information Literacy Series. Berkeley Heights, N.J.: Enslow Publishers, Inc., 2009.

**Gilbert, Sara.** *Write Your Own Article: Newspaper, Magazine, Online.* Write Your Own. Minneapolis: Compass Point Books, 2009.

# INTERNET SITES

FactHound offers a safe, fun way to find Internet sites related to this book. All of the sites on FactHound have been researched by our staff.

Here's all you do:

Visit *www.facthound.com*

Type in this code: 9781429661256

 Check out projects, games and lots more at **www.capstonekids.com**

# INDEX

# ABOUT THE AUTHOR

Jennifer Fandel received her Masters of Fine Arts degree in creative writing from Minnesota State University, Mankato. She has published more than 30 children's and young adult nonfiction books. Her book *The Light Bulb* received the Bologna Ragazzi Honorable Mention for Nonfiction at the 2005 Bologna Children's Book Fair. She loves to travel, bicycle, read, and (of course!) write.